D0832588

DISCARDED

ABOUT THE AUTHOR

Dr Aaron Balick is a clinical psychotherapist with twenty years of experience. He has taken the amazing insights from psychology out of the consulting room and made them accessible to the wider world. He has been an 'agony uncle' on CBBC and BBC Radio 1 as well as a mental health expert on television, online, and in print. He speaks internationally, offering a better understanding of the psychology of everyday life.

Aaron lives in London where he is the director of an innovative psychology hub, Stillpoint Spaces.

THE LITTLE BOOK OF

CALM

Tame your anxieties,
face your fears
and live free

DR AARON BALICK

LONDON · SYDNEY · AUCKLAND · JOHANNESBURG

1 3 5 7 9 10 8 6 4 2

Rider, an imprint of Ebury Publishing,
20 Vauxhall Bridge Road,
London SW1V 2SA

Rider is part of the Penguin Random House group of companies
whose addresses can be found at global.penguinrandomhouse.com

Penguin
Random House
UK

First published by Rider in 2018
www.penguin.co.uk

A CIP catalogue record for this book is available from the British Library

ISBN 9781846045547

Printed and bound in Great Britain by Clays LTD, St Ives PLC

Penguin Random House is committed to a sustainable future
for our business, our readers and our planet. This book is
made from Forest Stewardship Council® certified paper.

MIX
Paper from
responsible sources
FSC® C018179
www.fsc.org

INTRODUCTION

Sometimes life can be a struggle, and finding calm in the face of life's challenges doesn't always come naturally. Once we accept that these challenges *are* life, not something apart from it, we can meet them with equanimity.

As a psychotherapist with twenty years of experience, I've worked with hundreds of people to help them find this equanimity in relation to their life's challenges. I have learned that there's no magic bullet that works for everyone. The trick is to find strategies that work for you, and the rest is about acceptance.

I have also learned that most people underestimate their capacities to meet their life's challenges. I never cease to be amazed by what people can accomplish when they let go of their imagined limits to face their possibilities with an open heart.

This book is drawn from my experiences across the years of working with people to help them find the resources they need, not only to meet life's challenges, but to revel in them. Different approaches speak to different people, so I suggest you find the ones that ring true for you.

Each section offers either an accessible suggestion or technique to help you find calm, or a different way of seeing the world that may better enable you to accept life's difficulties as they come along. Each suggestion comes straight from clinical experience, the latest research, psychology and philosophy, or via the mouths of those much wiser than I.

Read the book straight through or open to a page at random. Think on it, practise it, and find your calm.

'All shall be well, and all manner
of things shall be well.'

JULIAN OF NORWICH

WHAT IS ANXIETY?

Anxiety is universal. It's an uncomfortable and unnerving feeling of worry or concern. Often we feel anxious about an actual thing, but anxiety can also be free-floating or undirected.

Most of us experience anxiety about something that might happen in the future (anticipatory anxiety) or about something that happened in the past (retrospective anxiety).

On a more profound level there is 'existential anxiety' – those discomfiting feelings we have about our place in the world, the meaning of life, big life choices, change, ageing, and the knowledge that someday we will die.

While it is natural to feel anxiety occasionally, it can impact negatively on your life if you feel it constantly or especially strongly. Sudden bouts of anxiety are called panic attacks.

The good news is that you don't need to be powerless in the face of your anxiety. You can learn to control it, and some of the ways to do that are actually quite simple. You can also learn to expand your tolerance of anxiety, so when you do experience it, it isn't so bad.

Anxiety can be a fact of life — but by keeping it in perspective, it doesn't have to get in the way of you enjoying your life.

'What does not destroy me
makes me stronger.'

FRIEDRICH NIETZSCHE

CORTISOL, ADRENALINE, AND NOREPINEPHRINE

These hormones are the holy trinity of stress. They are behind the butterflies in your stomach and the buzzing in your brain.

Adrenaline and norepinephrine work together towards your 'fight or flight' response. You can literally feel them pumping into your chest when you've been given a good scare.

Cortisol is slower to kick in but similarly prepares your brain to be awake for life's challenges. If we're stressed a lot, our levels of cortisol can remain high.

While our bodies mean well by producing these hormones to prepare us for life, more times than not they overestimate the threat — and we get worked up for nothing.

By learning to respond to stress triggers in better ways, we can also train ourselves not to overreact, which means a calmer response to just about everything.

WORK YOURSELF UP, OR WORK YOURSELF DOWN

Whenever you find yourself getting wound up and anxious about something, you can go one of two ways: work yourself up, or work yourself down.

Next time you notice your worrying thoughts swirling around with images of disaster lining up in some sadistic competition to scare you witless, you can be sure you're working yourself up. You'll know this because your breathing will be faster, your heart rate will increase, and you'll be thinking thoughts at the speed of an Olympic velodrome champion. That's your sign to stop.

Don't work yourself up: work yourself down instead. Slow down the breath, pause the thoughts, and dim out the images. This takes an act of will. Get in the way of your runaway mind and work your way down.

GOOGLE EARTH YOURSELF THE HELL OUT OF THERE

When you're anxious your worries take up all the space in your head – they become everything. When this happens, it's time to Google Earth yourself the hell out of there.

Close your eyes and imagine seeing yourself from above like in Google Maps. Then zoom out and see yourself getting smaller and smaller. See your home, then pan out slowly to your neighbourhood, and further again to your town or city, your country, your hemisphere.

Go right off the planet now, past the moon, beyond the solar system, and shoot out into space until Earth is a tiny speck that soon disappears.

This is a great exercise to make you feel very small and insignificant, but in a good way. Soon your worries will feel like that too.

THE MAGIC FORMULA

It is said that when it comes to anxiety, there is a magic formula.

ANXIETY =

overestimating how
bad something is going to be

×

underestimating how well you
think you can cope with it.

Now let's break that down a bit.

How bad *you think* something is going to be is not the same as how bad it will actually turn out. It's human nature to anticipate the worst just so you'll be prepared for it. But instead of helping, this level of intense anticipation paralyses us.

We also tend to *underestimate* how well we'll be able to cope with a challenging situation when it does arise. In fact, most people cope surprisingly well with almost anything that happens to them. It's *thinking* they won't be up to it that causes anxiety.

In short, you create your own anxiety by unconsciously doing the maths of the magic formula by saying 'It'll be terrible and I can't cope!'

Remember, it's hardly ever likely to be as bad as you anticipate, and you will find a way to cope with it – however difficult it may be.

So next time you experience anxiety, check the formula and redo the maths in your favour.

BEND IT LIKE BUFFY

In the TV show *Buffy the Vampire Slayer* a teenage girl faces real monsters as a metaphor of the horror of high school.

In one episode the demon Fear Itself is summoned. He attacks by making one's worst fears a reality. Buffy and the gang have to face their fears to vanquish this terrifying demon.

When he finally arises, we find he's not terrifying at all, only a tiny squirt, a few inches tall. More like Jiminy Cricket than a Hell Beast.

Buffy triumphs by simply squishing him under the toe of her stiletto.

'Big overture, tiny show,' exclaims sidekick Xander.

Remember Xander's words: Fear's bark is worse than its bite.

'He who fears he shall suffer,
already suffers what he fears.'

MICHEL DE MONTAIGNE

RIDE THE ROLLER-COASTER OF LIFE

Anxiety and excitement are closely related: it's just a matter of perspective. Some people love stepping out in front of a big crowd to perform, while others are terrified.

If your body 'reads' the feeling as fear, you'll be anxious. If it reads it as an adventure, you'll feel excitement. This is why some people love roller coasters and horror flicks – they get what is called a 'safe adventure'.

When you look at life as an adventure, you can change your feelings of fear into excitement. No excitement is without fear – but that's what makes it fun.

Seeing life like a roller coaster makes those dips appear less scary. It may seem crazy, but you could actually learn to enjoy them.

'I get up, I walk, I fall down.
Meanwhile I keep dancing.'

HILLEL

THIS TOO SHALL PASS

'Give it time' or 'time heals everything' are old clichés. It's just not what you want to hear when you're in the middle of feeling awful, because right now everything sucks!

Well let's re-work it.

'Giving it time' isn't about waiting until things get better. It's about knowing that all feelings pass.

Nobody likes throwing up, but everybody knows that they feel better afterwards. It's gross and unpleasant while it's happening, but avoiding it only prolongs the pain.

The uncomfortable feeling is inevitable, but it will come and it will go. Don't make it worse by anticipating, avoiding, and delaying. See it through. See it done.

WRITE IT DOWN

In psychology we have learned that 'externalising' — getting something out of your system — often makes us feel much better. It's those needling, worrying conversations in your head that are really torture.

Apart from speaking to someone about your worries, one of the best ways of externalising them is to write them down.

Don't try to solve the worries, justify or understand them. Just get them out of your mind and onto the paper. You don't even need to read them, so don't be shy.

This exercise works very well before bed, to help you leave them aside before sleep. Others find it helps first thing in the morning to clear out all the cobwebs before meeting the day fresh.

BE HERE NOW

These three simple words convey a great deal of wisdom passed down through thousands of years of Eastern philosophy. The tradition of this philosophy advocates the practice of awareness called mindfulness meditation.

'Be here now' recognises that we suffer when we focus our thinking on the past or the future instead of right now. Ask yourself honestly, is your anxiety about what's happening to you right here right now, or is it concern about yesterday or tomorrow?

The practice of being here right now is harder than it sounds, but you can start by reminding yourself, when you notice your now moment is polluted by thinking about the future or the past, to gently stop. Be here now instead.

'If you are depressed, you are living in the past. If you are anxious you are living in the future. If you are at peace you are living in the present.'

LAO TZU

GET UP AND GO

When feeling anxious or depressed you're likely to feel that your 'get up and go' has 'got up and gone'. You know you should get off your bum and get out into the world, but your body resists.

When it comes to 'get up and go' you simply have to stop thinking about it and do it. You have to will it, you have to be it, you have to get up and go. It doesn't matter how far, or how long it lasts, just show yourself you can get out the door.

Stop thinking about it! Just put your shoes on and go. Once you get out you'll see how much of your resistance was just in your head.

TURN THE COAT HOOK UPSIDE DOWN

Coat hooks are shaped that way because they are perfect for hanging things on. Were that hook to be upside down, things would slide right off it.

The thing that makes you anxious is the thing that's hanging on your psychological coat hook.

So, try to wonder what it would be like if you turned it upside down and let that thing or things just slip off.

Imagine feeling the weight dropping off as it slides down your psychological shoulders. It's a trick of the mind, to know how to turn it around, but once you learn it, and trust it, it's easy.

First, notice the worry is hanging there. Then flip it upside down and feel the weight come off.

NATURE, NATURALLY

Urbanites are missing out on something pretty important: greenery. It's no accident that the go-to images for 'calm' are rolling green countryside and the ocean. Research indicates that getting out into the green can do you a world of good.

Many of us who live in cities are accustomed to the constant ringing of sirens, the buzz of cars and buses, and the flashing of lights. But being accustomed to it doesn't mean there's no consequence.

We're also overstimulated by pinging emails, ringing phones, fluorescent lights, and a never-ending to-do list.

Keep yourself topped up with regular doses of greenery by way of lunch breaks and afternoon or morning walks. When you get the chance, go for mega-doses – long weekends, walking holidays – it's a sure way to feel calm.

DON'T ACCEPT
THE INVITATION

It may surprise you, but often anxiety can be a choice. When a worrying thought arises in your mind, it's like an invitation to become anxious. But what if you just didn't accept the invitation?

That arising thought may be something like:

- Did I offend so and so last night?
- Tomorrow's presentation is going to be a disaster!
- I think I left the iron on at home.
- S/he hasn't texted me since yesterday.

When a thought like one of these sends us an invitation to worry, we can politely decline, and slide it right back across the table. It's like saying, 'Thanks anyway, but I'm not going.'

FEEL YOUR WALK

Walking can be more than just about getting from point A to point B.

When point A is stressful and point B is super-stressful, walking ceases to be walking, it's just mulling over our disquiet and stress from one point to the next.

Why not use the journey as an opportunity? It doesn't have to be complicated or difficult. Simply feel your walk.

Notice how your feet touch the ground, how your body weight shifts to rhythm. Now slow it down and look around you. Stay with your walk, not whatever happened at point A or what might happen at point B.

By feeling your walk you take calm back for yourself. You integrate it into your day. It's simple. It's powerful.

THE BEDSIDE LIST

It's been an intense day and you can't sleep because you're unable to turn off all the thoughts swirling around your head.

When we don't prepare ourselves for shutdown, our anxious minds take it upon themselves to control us.

Part of what your mind is doing is making sure you don't miss anything. By 'catching' everything you can on paper (not on a screen, this is important) you reassure your mind that you can deal with those things tomorrow when you have the capacity.

So next time you're tormented, get out of bed, grab your bedside list and write down every little thing on your mind that you can deal with tomorrow. Pack it away in a drawer, and get some shut-eye.

TRUST

The source of much anxiety is a lack of trust: trusting that things will be OK or get better again; trusting that you can handle things when they go wrong; trusting others to help out.

When things have gone wrong for us we can lose trust all together. What's worse is that we find stories from our lives to back up why we shouldn't trust – ourselves or others.

What would it be like to trust again? To trust that you will recover? To trust that somebody's got your back? To trust that things just might be OK?

Trust is built up by trying it out, piece by piece with ourselves and with others. Don't give up on trust. Trusting can be enormously liberating.

'Sometimes I go about with pity for myself
and all the while the Great Winds are
carrying me across the sky.'

OJIBWE SAYING

NIGHTCAP

Many of us reach for a drink to deal with anxiety or stress. While the odd tipple here and there can be a pleasure – using alcohol to manage your feelings has consequences, like *increasing* anxiety.

After drinking, the combination of dehydration, bad sleep, and nasty toxins in your blood can leave your body feeling queasy and unsettled.

Because you're physically already ropey, your mind follows – feeling skittish, uneasy, and worried. If you've had an especially heavy night, you might be worrying about what you've said or done.

Letting your hair down occasionally can be a way to let off steam. However, if you find yourself needing alcohol regularly, you may be self-medicating, which will ultimately make you feel worse.

GO WITH THE FLOW

There are plans, and then there is reality. When reality gets in the way of plans, you need to go with the flow of reality.

For example, you plan to be there on time, even leaving plenty of time to get there. But something happens. A water main breaks, or the wrong kind of leaves have delayed your train. What to do?

You can resist the reality, but that won't get you there faster. Your resistance will only create frustration and unhappiness. Getting there on time is a ship that has already sailed.

When reality gets in the way of your plan, abandon the plan and reboot. It's not what you wanted, but it is what it is, so don't fight it.

SAVE BED FOR BEDTIME

Getting enough good sleep is crucial to a calm mind. Ideally, the bedroom should be used for little else than sleeping. Make a connection in your brain that bed means bedtime.

The rest of 'life' should be banned from the bedroom. Most importantly, your devices – mobile phone, tablet, computer – should be parked well outside the door.

The most that should accompany you to bed is a partner (if you have one) and a book (ideally, not a very exciting one).

Go to bed when you're ready, and leave the bedroom shortly after you've awoken. Your bedroom should be your temple of sleep. Treat it as such – sleep well – and you'll be in a great position from the moment you wake up to meet your day.

MONEY SECRET:
GET SECURE

Money can cause a great deal of anxiety and disquiet. Especially when there's not enough of it.

In this condition the primary objective is security. To get secure you have to face your fears and find out what's going on. Yes, open those envelopes and read those bank statements.

What's coming in and what's going out?

Money is numbers, and numbers can change. You just have to control them so they don't control you. It can be scary but fear is conquered by knowing what's happening.

When you know, you can plan, and planning feels good, especially when you start seeing the results. By knowing and doing (not worrying) you'll move from insecurity to security.

STEP ASIDE

When you feel like you're right at the centre of your own emotional storm, stepping aside helps you to gain control and perspective.

When you're in a state of high anxiety it's like those worries *are you* rather than a series of thoughts and feelings you're experiencing.

Imagine your anxiety as a cartoon brawl – a cloud of chaos storming around. You're in the middle of that chaos. Now, just step aside. The cloud of chaos is still there, but you're next to it, observing it more calmly.

Gaining an *aside* perspective is amazingly effective. While it might not resolve the source of your worries – it can give you the space you need to approach them more serenely.

EXERCISE

Hands down, exercise is the best medicine. Obviously for physical health, but for your brain too. It creates a healthy brain, lifts mood, and quells anxiety.

Studies have shown that regular exercise can work as well as antidepressants, and you don't need to be a gym bunny to feel the benefits.

The busier we get, the more likely we are to neglect physical activity. So next time you notice stress levels increasing and you haven't been moving about much – it's time to sweat – even just a little.

Occasional moderate aerobic exercise is enough to make a substantial difference. Grab it where you can – walk a bit more, go for a run, or get an active hobby. If you can take it outside then all the better.

GIGO (GARBAGE IN, GARBAGE OUT) 1

Since it's up to your mind to manage your worries, your brain should be in tip-top shape to do that.

As they say, 'garbage in, garbage out', so if you don't nourish yourself well, you'll feel like rubbish.

These things should be on your watch list:

- Sugary foods (and sugar-free substitutes)
- Too much caffeine
- Overdoing alcohol
- Tobacco
- Recreational drugs
- Junk food

Each of these things not only influences your body, but your mood too. By making sure you monitor what goes in you can minimise and make manageable any anxieties trying to come out.

PROGRESSIVE BODY RELAXATION FOR SLEEP

Having trouble sleeping? Get out of your head and into your body. Focusing on one part of your body at a time, progressively, is the way to do it.

Lying on your back, start with your feet. Take a long, slow breath in while squeezing your toes as hard as you can. As you release the tension, let the breath flow out and feel the stress leaving your toes and the feeling of relaxation coming in.

Now do the same with your foot, then with your shin, calves, knees, all the way up your body. You'll notice that the parts of the body you've already done feel like they disappear.

As you progress, you trade stress for calm, and pave the way for a long night's sleep.

WALK IT BACK

When you're in a state of reaction — what many of us call 'freaking out', it's like being on autopilot but in a bad way. We cycle through thoughts about the things we are worried about, generally making things worse.

This is the time to walk it back.

There is a moment where a choice can be made. We can run forward into what seems like a fierce fire, or we can pause, and slowly walk back from the heat.

This doesn't mean that the event is any less real or important; we just approach it in a different way. We slow down. We take a break, and we become less identified with the panic and better able to cope.

CLIMB UP A WALL
(LITERALLY)

It's pretty hard to worry about anything when you are clinging to a wall fifty metres up – and that's the whole point. Sure it's scary, but it focuses you like nothing else and has a surprising capacity to still the mind.

By joining a climbing club you can be assured that you're safe – the ropes will catch you if you fall. *You* know that, but your body doesn't and this provokes you to concentrate on one thing – sticking to that wall.

It doesn't have to be climbing – but any physical activity that requires you to be completely focused will put your everyday worries aside, while you concentrate on what's in front of you.

EXPAND YOUR
COMFORT ZONE

Imagine drawing a giant circle around yourself. Inside that circle you put everything you are comfortable with and, outside it, everything that makes you uncomfortable. These are your comfort zones.

Inside that circle are your routines, the people you know best, and the stuff you're good at. Outside it are unfamiliar things, people you are unfamiliar with, and the things you're not so good at.

The closer you get to the edge the more uncomfortable you feel.

By expanding your comfort zone and pushing the edge of that circle further out, the bigger your comfort zone becomes, and what was once uncomfortable will gradually become familiar.

Your personal growth lies at the edge of your comfort zone. Don't let fear hold you back. Go to the edge, and push it further out.

Come back to your centre to recharge. Breathe, ground yourself, and find your calm. Next time you step out that far you'll see your comfort zone has expanded — and so has your zone of calm.

'Nothing in life is to be feared,
only to be understood.'

MARIE CURIE

AVOIDANCE
(THE GOOD KIND)

Sometimes you can simply hit your limit. You can take only so much stimulation before you run out of the resources you need to deal with it. The trouble is, you keep ploughing forward: you just can't let go. This is the time for distraction (the good kind).

Get away from the situation. Take a walk. Watch a movie, even if it's the middle of the afternoon. Start cooking. Whatever it is, get off that one-track mind.

Sometimes it really is best to come back to it later. In the meantime, give yourself a little time away, so you can meet the challenge better when you're ready.

AVOIDANCE
(THE BAD KIND)

While stepping away from a situation can give you just the distance you need to attack it in a more productive way, avoiding too much does just the opposite.

Avoidance includes things like pretending something isn't happening; ignoring information you need to know; avoiding things that remind you of the worrying situation; pretending everything is OK.

A good example of avoidance is a pile of post you're not opening because of what you fear is inside. While it may be scary, the problem won't go away on its own.

Get an ally and hold somebody's hand when facing the scary thing. In the end, it's better to know, and to face it.

LEAN IN

If you've ever ridden a motorcycle you'll know that you have to lean into a bend. It seems counter-intuitive — your whole body wants to lean out! But leaning out of a bend throws everything off balance.

Leaning in means accepting that life at the moment is in a bend. Try as you might, leaning away only throws things even more out of balance and sometimes into a wobble or a tailspin.

By leaning in you accept the nature of this particular bend, and throw yourself into it. The asphalt might look very close — but every bend comes to an end, and then the motorbike will right itself.

HAVE AN ALLY

It may be a cliché, but it's true. A problem shared really is a problem halved.

One of the more difficult aspects of confronting worry is doing it alone. If you know that someone, even just one person, is on your side, it makes a huge difference.

If you're facing a particularly difficult or worrying challenge, it's time to lean on an ally. Find a person you trust and who won't judge you for your troubles. Ask them to help you through this rough time, and get them to check on you now and then as you face this challenge.

Don't be shy to ask.

One day you'll return the favour.

'Let us be grateful to people who make us happy, they are the charming gardeners who make our souls blossom.'

MARCEL PROUST

WATCH THE VIDEO

We watch videos because we get to experience the excitement of what's happening from the safety of the sofa. Sometimes doing this in your head can take the bite out of distressing situations.

Often when we are remembering distressing events or anticipating difficult ones to come, it is like we are the star of our own psychological thriller.

Instead of being the star of the film, try watching the video instead. This bit of distance between *you* and the *event* may be just what you need to step out of your role, and find calm in the face of serious challenges.

ME TIME

I know, I know, a bath full of bubbles surrounded by burning candles, classical music, blah blah blah ... Still, it's a cliché for a reason. It works.

We burn out because of the weight of demands from ourselves and others. We want to be a good employee; a good parent; or just a good person, but what do we do for ourselves?

Everyone needs to recharge – but we do this in different ways. For some it's a Netflix marathon, for others it's snuggling up with a good book. It doesn't have to cost much, but it does have to give you what you need.

MONEY SECRET:
WHEN THERE'S ENOUGH

Research shows that having *enough* money does increase happiness quite a bit, but beyond that the increase is only small.

Enough is not having to worry about it every day and having ample reserve in case something goes wrong.

Once you're over that 'enough' bump, your security rises and you reach a grounded feeling that increases calm and contentment.

What decreases calm and contentment is when you start comparing yourself to others.

'Sure, I have "enough" but not as much as "so and so".' Starting down this track is a sure way to stress and discontent. By all means, try to improve your lot but there will always be somebody better off. So don't get hung up on competition.

BE SHORT-SIGHTED

Short-sightedness is when you can't see very well at a distance but things that are close by are crystal clear.

Paradoxically, when we get anxious we tend to do so about the future or the past, even though we experience anxiety in the now.

Things that have happened in the past are no longer under our control and things that *may* happen in the future are still unfixed. When we expend anxious energy worrying about either, it's an exhausting waste of time!

What we can do is pay attention to things going on right in front of our noses instead.

By taking care of what you can *right now* you can mend mistakes from the past or prepare for the future instead of worrying about it.

LIFE'S LIKE AN ASSAULT COURSE

It's all about perception.

If you're running a 100-metre dash, and you come across a hurdle, you'll be surprised and you'll curse the hurdle for being in the way.

If you're running the hurdles, you expect them just as part of the course.

Life is like an assault course – it comes with tyres we have to jump across, walls we have to climb, and mud we have to crawl through. By expecting these little adventures, they're not 'in the way'.

Approach them as a natural part of life, not something that gets in the way of it.

'There is a voice that
doesn't use words. Listen.'

RUMI

BREATHE

It's the oldest trick in the book. So old that we do it automatically. But when the shit really hits the fan it's time to go back to basics.

When we're anxious, our systems fill with stress hormones, our hearts beat faster, and our breathing shallows.

This is when you need to breathe consciously, helping to ground you and slow the whole system down.

Take a long breath in through the nose. Hold it in just a couple of seconds, and then let it out through the mouth.

Breathe in relaxation, and breathe out stress.

About five rounds of this should do the trick, bringing you down from reactive anxiety into a place where you can get a better perspective.

LET'S DO THE TIME WARP AGAIN

Next time you're in a state of anxious worry, ask yourself, 'Am I going to care about this in a year's time?'

It turns out that 97 per cent of the stuff we are worrying about right now is of no consequence to us a week later, much less a year or five years away.

Think about something that had you shaking with anxiety a year ago. Perhaps something you said or did that you regretted. Is it so pressing now?

While some things will of course matter later in the future, the vast majority of our daily sufferings dissolve away. So why suffer?

Do the time warp, see the big picture, then ask yourself, 'Is it worth it feeling this way?'

IMMUNISE YOURSELF AGAINST NEGATIVE EMOTIONAL CONTAGION

Emotional contagion is when you get affected by an emotion that's happening in a larger group. If you cavort with complainers, you'll see what's wrong with stuff everywhere. If you work with worriers, well, worry you will.

If you can, the best cure for negative contagion is to find an emotional culture that's brighter and more positive. Try to hang out with people who reflect positivity and support.

If you can't shift away so easily, try to minimise your exposure to the negativity as best you can, and when it comes, don't add to it. Over time, build others into your social networks who can be allies in building a more positive culture.

TURN YOUR VELCRO
SUIT INSIDE OUT

Ever notice those things that just stick to you?
Something somebody said that still bothers you
even though they said it ages ago?

It's like you're wearing a Velcro suit, and
some people throw the kind of Velcro balls that
stick right to it.

Since you can't stop people throwing sticky
balls, turn your suit inside out instead. When
you do that, the balls don't stick: they just
fall off.

You'll be surprised what a relief it is to turn
that suit inside out and watch those balls just
bounce right off. Whether they stick or not is
now entirely up to you.

SLOW IT DOWN

When you find yourself frenetically looping in your head – thinking thoughts, stressing out, creating to-do lists – it's time to slow your pace – your *total pace*.

When we're frenetically trying to juggle a thousand things, it can feel like we're doing the right thing because we're so charged up, multitasking and working fast. Operating on overdrive is fine every now and then, but it's not for every day.

Next time you notice you're operating on speed dial, do something very simple. Slow your pace. If you're catching up on your emails, or digging frantically through drawers looking for a missing thing, slow it all down.

If you're thinking, calculating, making a Powerpoint presentation, it doesn't matter.

Slow your pace. It's better.

JUST NOTICE

We can often get carried away by our thoughts or our feelings. There's a big difference between having a passing thought or feeling and being totally possessed by that thought or feeling – especially if it's a disturbing one.

The fact is we are neither our thoughts nor our feelings. We simply *experience them*. It's our fear of experiencing them that makes them scream for attention.

So just notice them. This can be as simple as 'I notice I'm scared' or 'I notice I'm upset'. When you allow yourself to have the feeling, the feeling doesn't have to work as hard to get noticed so it stops knocking loudly on your door.

CHARM IN YOUR POCKET

Disturbing thoughts and feelings that are in your head can feel nebulous and hard to pin down. After all, you can't package up an uncomfortable feeling and tie it off neatly. You can, though, direct your attention elsewhere.

This works by transferring intangible worries in your head into a physical feeling between your fingers.

Whether it's prayer beads, a worry doll, a stress ball, or a rabbit's foot – some people find that having something around to hold in moments of worry brings calm.

The feeling of a physical object between your fingers grounds you in the here and now, rather than the abyss of your frightened mind.

What can you keep in your pocket?

PRIMITIVE FEARS
IN MODERN LIFE

Evolutionary psychology teaches us that the same fear response that was built in to protect us from wild animals is at work today — but most of what we're scared of won't kill us.

The things that *do* frighten us — failing a test, screwing up at work, embarrassing ourselves in public — scare us *as if we are encountering a wild animal* — even though the consequences aren't likely to damage us.

Sometimes it helps to remind ourselves that 99.9 per cent of the time the thing that we're afraid of is not life-threatening. So put your fears in perspective. It'll never be as bad as an encounter with a grizzly bear.

'We cannot see our reflection in running water. It is only in still water that we can see. The same is true with the mind.'

ZEN SAYING

ASK YOURSELF
WHAT YOU NEED

Sometimes we forget to ask ourselves the simplest question, 'What do I need right now?'

Being caught in a moment of great worry often makes us forget to make sure our basic needs are covered. We forget to ask ourselves simple questions like, 'Am I hungry? Am I cold? Do I need emotional support?'

In order to deal with our most pressing real-world concerns, we need to support ourselves first. It's not selfish, it's absolutely necessary. We need a firm ground to stand on before conquering our fears. Sometimes those needs are basic like sleep, nutrition, or even just a glass of water.

So next time you're caught up in what's going on out there – check that you have what you need in here.

MY WAY

Follow the advice from the Great Oracle at Delphi and 'know thyself'. Look deep inside and approach any given challenge in your life by drawing on the knowledge of what makes you tick.

While it's great to look to models and mentors to understand how to deal calmly with challenges, ultimately you will have to do it your way.

What are your skills and how can you utilise them best?

What do you find hard, and where can you find support?

Your world is in harmony when you approach life's challenges in a way that's congruent with who you are.

Others will do it their way – so do 'my way' with great respect – but find your way from an authentic place.

'The beginning is always today.'

MARY SHELLEY

GRATEFUL

We often get worried and anxious because we feel like something is missing. This is called a scarcity mentality. We experience it when we feel there's not enough time, money, love, status, or something else.

This anxiety can be so familiar that when it goes for a moment we might ask ourselves, 'Wait, I know I should be worrying about something – what is it?'

Don't look for it. This is toxic thinking.

STOP. Look the other way.

If you focus your attention on scarcity you will continue to feel you're lacking something inside: you're not.

Instead ask: 'What is in my life that I can feel grateful about today?'

The kind smile at the sandwich shop.

The way I can see the first spring buds on the trees outside my work window.

That I once had the opportunity to experience this wonderful memory.

That I have such a wonderful person in my life.

The way the wind blew though the oak leaves just now.

When you spiral out on negative thoughts you are in a scarcity mentality and need to find abundance.

Find substance in gratitude – remember what you have, and send your toxic thinking to the dump.

By shifting your attention to gratitude, you let the other stuff go.

When you smell the fresh air of gratitude, abundance will follow.

YOUR LITTLE TOE

Think about your little toe. Right now, just think about it.

Now you're aware of your little toe but were you aware of it before? Probably not. Where was it the whole time?

This is how focus works. When we're anxious or worried our focus is hijacked from us and pulled towards distressing thoughts. Then we passively follow that thought and feel distressed!

By learning to control our focus we can wrest back control of our thinking, and our suffering. It's you in charge, not your worry.

When you think of your little toe, you're not thinking about that worrying thing.

Pull yourself out of worry by changing focus. It doesn't have to be your little toe, but it's a start.

CATASTROPHISING

Psychologist Albert Ellis used clear and simple language like the word 'catastrophising' to describe the things we do to make ourselves miserable.

We catastrophise when we think about a future event as if it's going to be a total disaster. We get all worked up over a *story* we tell ourselves rather than the facts.

The cure for catastrophising is quite simple. Avoid it by sticking with the facts you know instead of speculating about a disastrous future. Think of a guy in the street who sees your furrowed brow and says, 'Hey, it may never happen!'

He might be right. But even if it *does* happen, it probably won't be as bad as you anticipate *and* you'll be able to cope with it better than you expect.

'Man is not worried by real problems
so much as by his imagined anxieties
about real problems.'

EPICTETUS

GET NEAT

Often our surroundings reflect what is going on in our heads. If your desk is a mess, so might be your mind.

No doubt some of us are neater than others. So it's important to judge your surroundings based on your own expectations. Are things messier than usual? Do you keep losing your house keys?

If you can't tidy up your mind first, start with your surroundings. Start with one room. Make a demonstration to yourself that you are taking control. A clean desk is a good start — so is a sparkling sink or bath.

Focus on the job of making things neat, and then enjoy the serenity. Now you've shown you can do that outside yourself, how about in your own head?

GET MESSY

While neatness may be a relief from a messy world, too much control can make us rigid and inflexible. If you can't be happy when there's just a pencil out of place, you'll have trouble in a world that can sometimes be pretty untidy.

If you need neatness to feel OK, how might it feel to try to be a bit messy on purpose? To leave the dishes in the sink overnight? To leave a small job undone? Horror!

For many, creating mess causes more anxiety, not less. But that's the point. If you can tolerate anxiety around your messiness, you can train yourself to do it about other things too. It widens your capacity to live with uncomfortable stuff.

Try it! You can always clean it up later (and you know you'll love it when you do).

LET IT BE

Feelings can arise spontaneously. Whether they are good feelings or bad ones, they just happen on their own and there's not much we can do about it. It's the same with thoughts.

Fighting a feeling almost always makes it worse. What if you could just accept it and let it be? No, it doesn't feel good, but it certainly feels less bad than fighting it.

By letting a feeling or a thought just be, we say to ourselves, 'OK, here I am having this feeling.' It might help to add 'and it's not the end of the world'.

While there are a lot of good tricks (including the ones in this book) on dealing with thoughts and feelings on *their level*, one of the single best ones you can learn is this one — to let them be.

Feelings come and go of their own accord, and the more used to that we become, the less distressing they will be.

BE YOUR OWN
SUPPORTIVE FRIEND

Often the times when we struggle the most are also the times we can be hardest on ourselves. We might say to ourselves, 'Get on with it', 'Pull yourself together' or 'Oh how could you be so stupid'. We can talk to ourselves in ways that we'd never speak to a friend. So why can't we treat ourselves like a supportive friend?

You wouldn't kick someone while they're down – so why should you kick yourself? When you catch yourself doing it, stop. Then speak to yourself as you would to the person you love most in the world.

If you're seeking calm, start by giving it to yourself.

LET IT GO

When you hold on to thoughts, memories, or conversations, they weigh you down.

Maybe it's time to let them go.

If you're able to make amends, make them. If you're able to get closure, try.

However, we can't always do those things, either because someone refuses to give it to us, or because that person is no longer with us.

When you can't fix it and when you can't change it, you have to let it go. Let yourself feel the weight lift, and the relief that comes from not having to hold it any more.

'It is what it is.'

UNATTRIBUTED

SOMEBODY ELSE'S SHOW

We often live our lives as if we're the stars of our own shows. The more we look inward, the lonelier we feel – like our show is the only story in the world.

This is the perfect time to think about other actors in all those other shows. Consider that the supporting actors in your show feel like the star performers in their own. And for them, you're a supporting act!

Then there are the billions of people you've never met, all starring in their own life show. It's easy to forget that everybody in the world feels the same way. When you realise this at a very deep level, it can be a great relief.

SECONDARY FEELINGS OF PRIMARY EMOTIONS

Did you know that when you experience anxiety or worry it is often a *secondary* feeling covering up a primary emotion?

When we find ourselves caught up in frenetic worry about things we have no evidence for — like our health, the safety of loved ones, imagined future disasters — that worry is often a proxy for a more primary emotion we are unaware of.

For example, while you may be worrying an awful lot about your health, despite doctors telling you you're OK, you might be hiding another concern from yourself. Perhaps about your relationship, your job, or a loved one.

Alternatively, you may find yourself concerned about what's going on at work, but unaware that there's something you want to say, strongly, and that frightens you.

Frenetic worry often gets in the way of serious messages we're getting from our system. By quieting the worry, we can get to the main emotion.

If it feels like a worry spiralling out of control, it won't help you. You have to step out of it first. Then, acknowledge that your anxiety is a red herring, and look instead for the real McCoy.

You're probably scared of the real McCoy, but don't be. Once you face it, you'll be on the road to dealing with it with a cool head.

LET'S GET PHYSICAL

Get out of your head and into your body. Do it like this:

Choose something that takes physical effort *and* control or precision: something you have to concentrate on to do correctly.

It might be yoga, martial arts, or dance. Find a good teacher. Get your attention out of your head and into your muscles, your form, your breath, your body.

When you're working on a pose, movement, or routine, it takes all your concentration. Move from head-brain to body-brain. You need this. It's good for you.

Yes, it's hard. But that's the point. Exercise other than from your mind.

Sure, your body will be sore the next day, but your monkey mind will have had a break.

DO SOMETHING HARD

It might seem counter-intuitive to do something hard in order to feel at ease. But it's not.

Finding calm isn't about doing nothing; it's about what you pay attention to, how you focus, and gain control over your thoughts.

Choose anything, a new skill, something that takes effort.

Learning to stick at something hard helps to train your mind.

The key is that you put your mind to something challenging and see it through.

Remember though, this isn't about torturing yourself! It's about bedding into the hard work of concentration and training your brain.

It's a paradox, but you'll find that the harder you concentrate, the quieter your mind will be.

'Courage is the price that life
extracts for granting peace.'

AMELIA EARHART

GO FLY A KITE

When conditions are right, it takes no effort to fly a kite. It flies itself. It's in a kite's nature to fly.

When a kite is doing what comes naturally, it's a metaphor for trust. It floats on the wind, and you anchor it. Even if it needs some help, a running start for example, once it gets in the air, it dances without effort.

You too are like a kite. When the conditions are right, you can soar. But what makes the right conditions?

The right kind of wind, you might say. But when that 'right kind of wind' isn't blowing does the kite care? No, it sits quietly on the ground without expectation – but when that wind comes, it soars. Naturally.

CLEAN DISHES/
DIRTY DISHES

You know that feeling of relief you get when you've done all the washing up and every dish is nicely stacked where it belongs?

Then, as if no time has passed, you see them in the sink covered in muck.

'How did that happen so fast?'

This is life. There are no clean dishes without dirty dishes. Dirty dishes must be washed to have clean ones. If you accept that clean dishes will always get dirty, why curse the time you spend cleaning them? It's just part of the cycle.

In life it's the same. Don't curse the part of your life spent cleaning metaphorical dishes.

Accept your dishes as they come – dirty and clean.

DON'T PAPER OVER
THE CRACKS

A good proportion of stress and anxiety isn't down to the actual problem, it's down to the way you approach that problem.

In fact, most stress in relation to a problem is about fighting the fact that there *is* a problem.

Often, when confronted with a difficulty, we try to paper over the cracks, or worse, ignore the cracks all together.

So, let there be cracks!

We all have cracks and we don't need to hide them. Instead of papering over them, see them as part of your personal landscape. Address what needs to be addressed, and leave the rest as they are.

Better a uniquely distressed wall, than layers of peeling wallpaper anyway.

THERE ARE 26.1 MILES BEFORE THE END OF A MARATHON

Goals are good things to have, but don't get hung up on them.

The goal is only at the very end of the project. It is the finish line. It is the final achievement. Don't hold your breath until the end. Don't feel like nothing matters until you get there.

There are 26.1 miles to run before the end of a marathon.

There are many years of study before someone hands you a degree.

There is a lot to be written before you reach the last page of a book.

There's much experience to be gained before landing the perfect job.

When we get hung up on goals themselves we miss everything along the way.

We work ourselves up for not getting there fast enough and we feel bad as we watch people around us reach their goals.

We've heard that it's all about the journey and not the destination, but we insist on driving ourselves nuts about destinations.

Feel that first mile, enjoy that first essay, write that first page, and invest in your work.

You spend a lot more time moving towards a goal than actually achieving it. So don't rush so much to get to the end.

'Think of all the beauty still left
around you and be happy.'

ANNE FRANK

'Life is a series of natural and
spontaneous changes. Don't resist them;
that only creates sorrow. Let reality be
reality. Let things flow naturally forward
in whatever way they like.'

LAO TZU

PUT ON YOUR
OXYGEN MASK FIRST

There's a reason why airline safety demonstrations ask you to put on your oxygen mask before assisting someone else. Should the cabin depressurise, it can take seconds to lose consciousness. So you need to keep your head so you can save another's.

Many of us give so much to others that we forget to look after ourselves. We spend our valuable resources on those we care about, leaving nothing for ourselves.

It's not selfish to put your oxygen mask on first, it's absolutely necessary.

This is, of course, a metaphor. But it's an important one. You will support others better when you are adequately supported yourself.

When's the last time you checked if your oxygen mask was on?

GET YOUR HANDS DIRTY

When you feel full of stuff – thoughts, conversations un-had, volatile emotions – it might be time to externalise. This means to get it out of your head. But where do you put it?

Making thoughts and emotions into something solid can really help. Get clay, mash it about, form something, get it under your fingernails.

Perhaps colour is more your thing. Grab crayons, chalk, pastels, finger paint! The thing is to get your hands dirty, get it out of your head, and onto paper.

Thoughts and emotions are elusive. A piece of art is a *thing*. Give yourself the opportunity to express your feelings into things, and find some calm on the other side.

CHANGE IT, ACCEPT IT, OR GET OUT OF THE WAY

When you confront a situation that you are unhappy with, you really have only three choices: change it, accept it, or get out of the way.

To change it you need to have the courage to try. Get all the help you can to make a situation better.

If it is truly out of your control then it cannot be changed. By accepting it you stop fighting the inevitable.

If you cannot change it, and you cannot accept it, you may have to get out of the way. This also takes courage because it might mean leaving a relationship, quitting a job, or taking another kind of risk. If it's impossible to get out of the way, then it's back to acceptance.

Accepting it or getting out of the way is not giving up. It is about taking a realistic view of a situation that is truly out of your control, and making a choice in your best interest.

PERISH THE THOUGHT
(LITERALLY)

Thoughts can make us suffer. We can follow them down dark alleys to places that make us feel dreadful, frightened, agitated, or furious. One way of dealing with thoughts is with other thoughts. You might say 'Don't worry, it's not so bad' for example. This is dealing with the thoughts on their own level.

Sometimes this works. Other times it just starts a back and forth that goes on in your head ad nauseam. Sometimes the best thing you can do is perish the thought.

But how do you get rid of a thought. Just see it for what it is: a thought. This is both very easy and very difficult. You see, you have to let that thought go, without overthinking it.

GIGO (GARBAGE IN, GARBAGE OUT) 2

Our first encounter with 'garbage in, garbage out' dealt with the physical stuff that can tip us into feeling not so hot. This time it's the mental stuff.

What is your brain consuming? A torrent of tweets? A phalanx of Facebook posts? A non-stop Netflix binge? More distressing news about the world? Are these things contributing to calm or to stress? Garbage in, garbage out.

What you consume mentally is as important as what you consume physically. Make good choices about what your brain encounters. Choose quality. Choose slow mental food. It will pay dividends.

SALTWATER FISH
IN FRESH WATER

Saltwater fish are so graceful and beautiful. Freshwater fish pale in comparison to those you'll find around the Great Barrier Reef.

Fancy saltwater fish don't last long in fresh water. They lose their lustre and become sickly. They need to be back in the right environment in order to thrive and survive – to return to grace.

Are you a beautiful saltwater fish trying to make it in fresh water? Maybe it's your job, your relationship, or the town you live in. Perhaps it's other circumstances that need to change.

We need to exist, if we can, in environments that enable us to thrive. By looking honestly at your environment – identify what needs to change. Make sure you've got the context you need in order to calmly shine.

PAIN VS. SUFFERING

There's pain, and there's suffering. Pain is usually unavoidable — like a sore tooth, or a broken heart. Suffering usually makes pain worse.

Getting a jab causes a small amount of pain. But if you anticipate that pain you'll suffer with anticipation, you'll suffer during the jab because you're more likely to tense when the needle goes in, and you'll suffer afterwards from the trauma of it all.

Isn't it better just to feel the pinch and be done with it? Pain, sure, but it's over quickly. No suffering.

Next time you're in pain, try not to suffer.

Pain is a part of life. Suffering doesn't have to be.

WEARING A WET NAPPY

Babies cry when they're uncomfortable. The very little ones don't even know why they're uncomfortable — they just feel rotten. Is it because of hunger? The need to burp? Or a wet nappy?

Look at the baby's face when the wet nappy is replaced with a clean, dry one. That's the face of calm.

Sometimes we're wearing wet nappies and we don't even know it. We walk around feeling uncomfortable, unhappy, stressed out, or worried, and don't even know it.

Maybe that wet nappy is a job undone, a relationship issue unresolved, a promise to the self not kept. Find out what your wet nappy is and change it. You don't have to walk around so uncomfortably any more.

THE PUPPY
UNDER THE BED

We can be quite nasty to ourselves sometimes. We tell ourselves off for not doing something well; we hate our bodies; or we make a mistake and then rip ourselves to pieces for it.

You might argue that if you weren't so mean to yourself you'd never get anything done. But is that the best motivation?

Imagine a scared puppy hiding under a bed. How would you get it out? Would you yell and scream and poke it with sticks? Of course not.

You'd treat it gently and compassionately until it feels safe enough to come out on its own.

That's how you should talk to yourself when you're anxious or struggling. Respect the part of yourself that's like a puppy under the bed, and treat it well.

DEVICE OVERWHELM

Are you recharging? No, I don't mean your smartphone, your laptop, or your smartwatch. I mean you.

Our environments are so full of distractions that we can go through long periods of paying attention to everything but ourselves. Notifications, emails, pinging this, buzzing that. Give it a break!

Our devices are built to distract us, which is the opposite of calm, so we need to not let them do that.

Find time each day to be away from your devices. If you're out for lunch, leave your phone behind. Ban devices from the bedroom and take them off the table when speaking to friends.

Devices contribute to your anxieties. Don't let them control you. You decide when.

'There is no living thing that is not afraid
when it faces danger. The true courage is
in facing danger when you are afraid, and
that kind of courage you have in plenty.'

THE WIZARD OF OZ, L. FRANK BAUM

BE AFRAID,
BE VERY AFRAID

Fear is fine. It activates us and gets us ready to meet challenges in life. When we avoid our fears or put them off, they gain power over us through avoidance (the bad kind), worry, and unease.

Most people are under the illusion that they will deal with a scary situation when the fear goes away. The thing is, if we don't confront the scary situation, we'll never challenge our fear.

Meet your fear head on.

- If it's a conversation, have it.
- If it's a decision, make it.
- If it's a deed, do it.

The fear will go *after* you've faced it, not before. So you might as well accept your fear, and face it.

DESCARTES WAS WRONG

'I think therefore I am.' Right?

Well, it certainly *feels* like that but people are *not* their thoughts. Still, thoughts have enormous power over our emotions. If we think a negative thought, we start to feel pretty negatively too.

If you think 'I'm a terrible person' you are likely to feel like one. But guess what, that's really just a thought. It could have been any other thought.

So replace that thought with something totally ridiculous like, 'I'm actually a furry elephant.' That is a thought just like the last one — only you know it isn't true.

Now you might just say, 'But it's true I am a terrible person.'

Guess what? The only thing that's true about it is that it's a thought. And you are not your thought.

ZONE OF CONTROL

Would you say that your 'zone of control' was inside or outside yourself?

While it's clear that many things are outside our control, much mental unrest comes from feeling out of control about the very things that we *could* be in control of.

Whether it's meeting deadlines, having difficult conversations, making healthy choices, or saving money, we routinely blame others for choices we should be making ourselves.

Look honestly at your zone of control – are you taking responsibility for your choices? The more you act from your centre – the calmer you will be in making your choices, and following them through.

TASTE YOUR FOOD

When's the last time you actually tasted your food? Like *really* tasted it: the flavours, the texture, the temperature?

Many of us eat to live, rather than the other way around. While we may remember to appreciate it when we sit down for a fine meal, what about that simple sandwich at lunch, or your snack in front of the computer?

Food is one of life's finest pleasures. Enjoy it.

By stopping to enjoy your food, you put a series of sensual breaks into your day. This is an important way of grounding yourself and reconnecting with your body.

Whether it's a snack, or a full-blown meal, stop and taste it. A greater calm and grounding will follow.

LET THE SUNSHINE IN

This one is literal. Let the sunshine in.

When the storm clouds collect over our heads, we can forget to look out the window and appreciate the sun.

In winter months, when there is a lack of sun, this can make things even worse. Summer or winter, direct sunshine on your skin is thought to brighten mood by increasing mood-enhancing neurotransmitters like serotonin.

When we're depressed or distressed we can withdraw into our dark caves. Meeting the sunshine means we have to go out. It's a signal to ourselves that we're seeking brightness.

When the sun peeks past those clouds get outside and let the sunshine in.

ALL CHANGE

There's no avoiding change, so why fight it?

Most of us get comfortable in our ways, and when we see change on the horizon we can become anxious. Change has the capacity to stir us up, to introduce the unexpected, and to make us fearful.

The trouble comes when we try to deny change, avoid it, or stop it. We become rigid in the face of the inevitable, and that makes us less able to cope with it.

Darwin showed us that the species which adapt to change are the ones that survive. For example, the tree that bends in the wind won't break in half — it's adapted to change.

You can't stop change, but you can adapt to it. See change as an exciting opportunity to adapt and grow.

'The only thing certain
is nothing is certain.'

MICHEL DE MONTAIGNE

MONEY SECRET: SPEND ON OTHERS, SPEND ON EXPERIENCES, NOT THINGS

If you're fortunate enough to be financially secure you might wonder what's next. Acquiring even more will not bring you the kind of happiness that becoming financially independent did. What's more, after a certain point, it has diminishing psychological returns.

The happiness derived from buying things is very short-lived.

Shared experiences are enjoyed and remembered much more than things are. Take your loved ones on adventures they'll remember for a lifetime.

Help other people or causes achieve their goals. Contribute to a culture of generosity.

Keep enough money to make you feel safe, but don't hoard it and don't get obsessed with more. Use the rest to inspire generosity in others and create the conditions of abundance for all those you can.

Will Rogers: 'Too many people spend money they earned ... to buy things they don't want ... to impress people that they don't like.'

SEE THE SEA

Unless you're lucky enough to live by the coast, this one takes a special trip, but it's worth it.

There is something about the expanse of the sea that has the unique power to cut across any sense of 'choppy waters' in one's own head. So see the sea, but do it with purpose.

Approach a quiet part of the coast where you won't be interrupted. Stand near the shoreline facing the horizon.

Feel the wind on your face.

Smell the salty air.

Listen to the sounds of the waves.

See the pattern of the waves as they approach you.

Let everything else go. Become what you are witnessing. Be there.

Now hold that thought, and take it with you.

WALKING MEDITATION

Walking meditation is like mindful pacing.

You can do it almost anywhere, indoors or out – just make sure it's quiet and you won't be interrupted.

Just like a sitting meditation, set yourself a time (ten minutes to start should do) during which you walk mindfully for just ten to fifteen paces. Stop. Breathe. And when you're ready, walk back, and stop to breathe again on the other side.

While you're walking mindfully notice your natural breathing, the weight of your feet on the ground, the way your body moves. If your thoughts wander, gently bring them back to your walk or your breath.

This improves with practice, so keep at it.

LOVE AND BE LOVED

Our relationships with others are one of the most important things about being human.

When we struggle in our lives we lean on those around us.

When things are going well, we celebrate our successes with them.

In turn we are leaned on, and we celebrate others' successes too.

For some of us being able to love and be loved doesn't come automatically. It takes work. Be gentle and curious with yourself if this is happening to you.

Think of those people in your life with whom you are closest. Think how much you care about them.

Tell them.

Care for them.

Love them.

FEEL THE EARTH
BENEATH YOUR FEET

This exercise is best done outside and in bare feet, so be mindful of where and when you choose to do it. It's most effective on natural grass.

Now take off your shoes and socks and feel the earth beneath your feet.

So much of our lives we're in comfortable (or not) shoes traipsing over smooth floors, being carried by escalators or lifts, or being zoomed around in cars and trains. When do we actually touch down?

Just stand on that uneven ground. Feel the weight of your body pressing on the balls of your feet. Imagine how far the land goes down below you, and the force of gravity on your body.

This is called grounding. Get connected. Get calm.

THAT GUILTY
MUSICAL PLEASURE

Think of that one song that you wouldn't be caught dead dancing to in public. Now find a private place (an empty bedroom usually does the trick) and play that music, loud, and dance.

We spend so much of our lives feeling inhibited – being socially compliant – doing the right thing, when we rarely express ourselves freely. There's a part of you that's dying to express itself, and now it's time to give it a chance.

Dancing to your guilty pleasure has the power to cut across feelings like stress or depression. It also works well for getting you to take yourself less seriously. You'll also feel remarkably calm afterwards.

Come on. It's time. What will your guilty pleasure be?

COME ON IN,
THE WATER'S COLD

Are you a toe-in-the-water-first or a dive-right-in kind of person? These are two very different approaches to life.

While it's wise to test the water, you're rarely going to find a pool that's just the right temperature. Sometimes you just have to leap.

Cold water is unpleasant at first, but it's not harmful: you get used to it.

Fear often keeps people from taking a plunge. Sometimes you need to allow yourself to be cold for a little while until you get the hang of it.

Are you loitering around the edge of the pool of life? Is that keeping you worried, consternated, or unsettled? Well, come on in! The water might be cold, but you'll feel better for having taken a leap.

SCREAMING BABY
ON A PLANE

Some of our worst worries are like a screaming baby on a plane. At first you can't ignore it, but after a while you don't hear it so loudly – the noise becomes part of the furniture. When it does finally stop, you realise how very quiet it is and experience enormous relief.

Our more abiding worries are like the screaming baby we've got used to. You don't hear the piercing cries any more, but it is likely to still be distressing you in the background.

Perhaps you notice the underlying stress of an abiding worry? If you can identify why your 'screaming baby' might be upset and then address it – you might be surprised just how quiet it can become.

TURN THAT GREAT DANE INTO A TOY POODLE

Sometimes you *know* your thought, worry, or fear is overblown, but you still can't seem to let it go.

In a situation like this your worrying thought is like a giant Great Dane pulling you down the street behind it by its leash: it has all the control.

However, if you could re-imagine this Great Dane as a tiny toy poodle, how scary is that?

This doesn't make the worry go away entirely – toy poodles are harmless, but they can yap like nobody's business.

But a small dog barking at the end of a leash is a whole different league of concern. Sure, you can hear it yapping away beside you, but it's *you* that's in control of the leash.

WHAT YOUR BODY NEEDS

How well do you listen to your body? I mean actually *listen* to it. Are you aware of when you're hungry, when you need a breath of fresh air, or even when you need to pee?

Our bodies need our attention, and when we don't give them that, they try to let us know.

Being mindful of the basics – that you're well fed, well watered, and well, erm, emptied – will provide you with a solid ground for a state of calm. Being unaware of your basic needs has knock-on effects that begin in a subtle way, but increase until you *have* to respond.

Don't let it get that way. Keep an ear to your body, and treat it well.

MEDITATION

If meditation were called 'sitting quietly with yourself' it would seem a lot less of a mystery.

Incorporating meditation into your life has a ton of benefits for your well-being – most notably for a general sense of equanimity and equilibrium. The simplest way to do it is to find time, every day, to sit somewhere quietly.

Focus on your breath and observe your thoughts and feelings without judgement. That's it.

By doing this regularly you get a slight distance from the din of your life, learning bit by bit that you are not your thoughts and you are not your feelings.

By silently watching them go by, you are less riled by both.

NIGHT SWIMMING

Try this sometime. Float under the stars.

You can do this in a swimming pool — but the effect is much greater if you can find a natural water source.

You can either float on your back or get some assistance from a lilo. Position yourself in a quiet place staring up at the sky.

Make sure your ears are underwater, so everything is beautifully muted. Now just look up at the stars as the water laps gently around you. You are fully supported looking up into the cosmos.

Just enjoy the sensation, and do nothing more than listen to the water, and possibly the sound of your heart. This is a treat. This is calm.

MUSIC

When is the last time you *really* listened to music? Not something in the background, and not something blaring from your earbuds when you're trying to take the edge off a commute.

These days we don't give music the attention it rightly deserves – a truly immersive experience at the expense of everything else.

When is the last time you just stopped and listened?

Do it now. Choose something gentle, harmonic, possibly something classical. My recommendation is 'The Moldau' or 'Vltava' from Smetana's *Má vlast*.

Listen to a whole movement. Close your eyes. Detach. Become the music.

TOP OF THE HILL

In *Dead Poets Society*, Robin Williams's character stands on his desk and encourages his students to do the same.

'I stand upon my desk to remind myself that we must constantly look at things in a different way. Just when you think you know something, you have to look at it in another way, even though it might seem silly, or wrong, you must try!'

This is good advice.

Try it from your desk, but I recommend a wider vista. A hill, a mountain if you're able. See the big picture. Your little view can feel rather squeezed and familiar at times, so this will give you a different perspective.

DON'T FIGHT THE NOW

One of the greatest sources of mental unrest is when you are fighting the now. This usually happens when you sense that a feeling you might be having will be unpleasant. These feelings might be:

- Loss
- Fear
- Feeling misunderstood

- Sadness
- Anger
- Loneliness

When we avoid the now moment, we are fighting against nature. While the feeling you are avoiding may indeed be unpleasant, trying *not* to feel that feeling makes the bad even worse.

Let go. Feel how you are feeling now. Let the feeling wash through.

The first thing you'll learn is that it's not so bad after all.

The second thing you'll learn is how much better you feel not fighting the now.

DO GOOD

One of the interesting things about worry and anxiety is that they are so egocentric. That means all of the thoughts and worries tend to swirl around what it means to ME.

Of course we often do a great deal of our worrying about others. But if you really dig down, you're likely to find that even those worries ultimately end up in your lap.

'What will it be like for *me* if such and such happens to *them*?'

Now we all get egocentric at times, it's natural. But when we are stirred up and under stress, it's especially important to tip that balance away from the ego.

It's time to do something good.

Your good can be anything, from a single good deed to setting yourself up for regular do-gooding by becoming a volunteer.

Whether it's cleaning up the environment, befriending someone, or giving a hand to someone less fortunate, it will de-centre yourself from your ego and reap benefits (and calm) for yourself and others.

Importantly, this has to be something you *do*. Setting up a direct debit is great, but for it really to work, you have to muck right in.

Help build an abundance mentality through giving and generosity. Giving to others and being for others sweeps away your shame and guilt while providing others with what they need.

Be altruistic, be good, be calm. It's no crime to feel better about yourself while you're giving back to others.